THANK YOU FOR
MY DREAMS

Also by Alexi Lubomirski

Princely Advice for a Happy Life
Diverse Beauty
Decade

THANK YOU FOR MY DREAMS

Bedtime Prayers of Gratitude

HSH Prince **Alexi Lubomirski** and sons

Andrews McMeel
PUBLISHING®

Introduction

I began consciously saying "thank you" when I was in my late twenties.

I became aware that whenever I felt down, sad, or angry about something (especially angry), I could feel the anger manifesting in my chest and stomach.

So I mentally said a prayer of thanks in an attempt to change my demeanor, and after a minute of concentrating on something I was grateful for, I very quickly noticed the physical changes in my body. Even though the initial problem still remained, I felt calmer and better equipped to deal with it.

Fast-forward fifteen years and I am married with two young sons. Every day I mentally say (pray) "thank you" for the things in my life, such as my health, my family, love, a home, a job, and everything else that I take for granted like legs that work, eyes that see, and ears that hear. It has become as important as meditation, exercise, or a cup of green tea. I simply feel better after doing it.

One night when he was four, my eldest son asked me what praying was and what I prayed about. I explained that saying "thank you" to God or the universe (or whatever he wanted to call it) was very important. So we started off slow: "Thank you for Mommy and Daddy."

A few months later, he had his first vivid nightmare. In his half-sleep state, he couldn't get out of the terror of his dream and kept falling back into it. Realizing that he could not change his emotion by himself, I suggested that we say our thank-yous. We said "thank you" for the family, for our dog, for his scooter, for chocolate chip cookies, for warm days in the garden, for swimming in the sea, for his legs so he could run fast. . . . After two minutes he was asleep and stayed that way for the rest of the night.

In the beginning, the boys struggled to think of more than five things each to be thankful for. Gradually it became easier, and one day, after one of our thank-you sessions, I decided to write down what they were thankful for, in their own words. My hope being that it would help other children open themselves up to the wonderful tool of just saying "thank you." ☺

For Giada,
the best mama and
wife in the world!

Morning

Thank-yous, as dictated by
Sole Luka and **Leone**

Thank you for letting us wake up
every morning when we feel happy and healthy.

Thank you for when Mommy and Daddy wake us up with kisses and we get to have morning cuddles in their bed before breakfast.

Thank you for my ears so that I can hear the voices of all the people I love and also so

Thank you for the sun that keeps us warm, helps plants grow, and helps give us electricity through solar power, without giving any pollution.

Thank you for the food in our bellies that keeps us healthy and strong.

7

Thank you for our tongues that help us to **taste** things like **vegetables**, **bananas**, and **spicy sauces**.

Thank you for our clothes
that keep our bodies warm.

9

Thank you for the oceans that are the home for **whales**, dolphins, swordfish, octopus, squid, crabs, and **seaweed** for them all to eat.

Thank you for our hair that keeps our heads warm.

Thank you for our brains that help
us to think and read and write.

Thank you for my feelings,
so that I know when I feel
happy or sad or angry or silly.

Thank you for all the animals on planet earth that are also our **brothers** and **sisters** and that have **feelings** too.

Thank you for making me brave when I am **scared** sometimes, like when I have to go to a **new school** or learn to **swim** or try new **food** that I don't think that I like.

Thank you for my skin so that
I can feel things like hot and cold water
and Daddy's tickles
and Mommy's kisses on my cheek.

Thank you for the feeling when I laugh because it makes me so happy and then I laugh more.

Thank you for all the faucets in our house that let us get water whenever we want to drink or wash. Some people don't have that, so we are very lucky.

Thank you for phones that let us talk to our family and friends when they are not in the same room.

Thank you for our smiles because it shows other people when we are happy. I like it when people smile when we pass them on the street.

Thank you for bees that help make all the plants grow

so we can have food to eat. Without bees there wouldn't be any food.

Thank you for teachers who teach us about life and how to read and write and to be kind to each other.

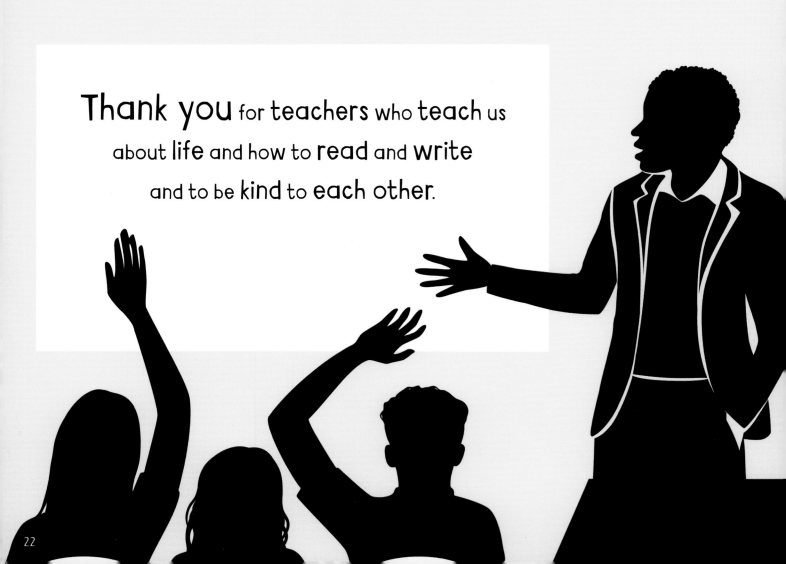

Thank you for our friends who make us laugh
and who make us feel better when we are sad

Thank you for that feeling I get inside my whole body when I feel love, like when Mommy and Daddy are smiling at me when I am not doing anything.

Thank you for my arms so I can hug,
hands so I can clap,
legs so I can run,
toes so I can balance,
knees so I can jump,
bones that hold me together,
and muscles that make me stronger!

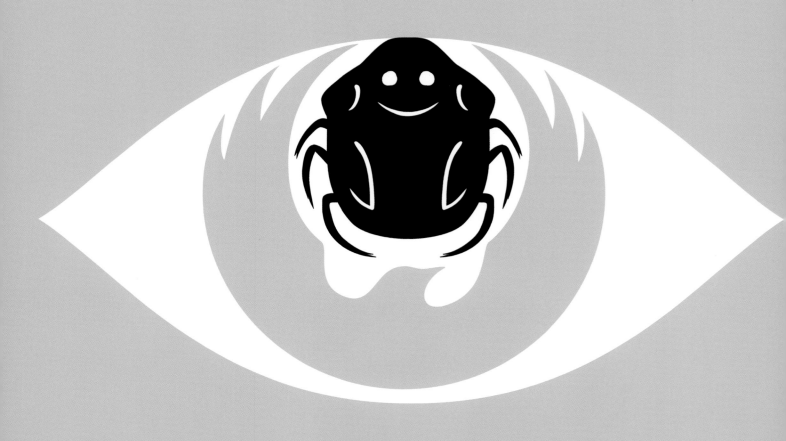

Thank you for our eyes so we can see all the beautiful things in the world like colorful birds, happy people, and funny insects.

Thank you that everyone has different-colored skin
and are different **shapes** and **sizes**. Lots of different **colors**
are **good** because it is like when you have lots of different-colored
crayons and you can make a **beautiful drawing.**

Thank you for all the colors
in the world.
My favorite color is . . .

Thank you for music because then we can dance
and sing and learn how to be in a rock band.

Day

Thank you for the **rain forests** that are **home**
for thousands of **birds**, **animals**, and **insects** and also for
making all the **oxygen** that we need to **breathe**.

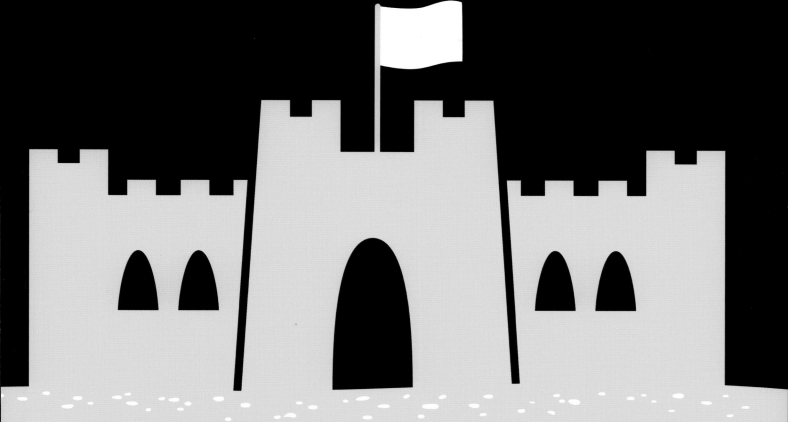

Thank you for beaches so we can play
in the sand and make castles.

Thank you for when the blossom grows on the trees because it makes the city look like a beautiful garden.

Thank you for people who invent things to stop pollution and for the garbagemen who take all the garbage away from our streets and they also take all our recycling away, which helps the planet.

Thank you for when **spring** comes because sometimes **winter** is too **long** and I just want it to be **spring**.

Thank you for our noses so we can smell all
the beautiful flowers and delicious food
that Mommy and Daddy make.

Thank you for firefighters who help
people get out of buildings that are on fire.

Sometimes they sleep at the fire
station so that they can quickly
go to a fire on their fire truck.

Thank you for doctors and hospitals who make us feel better when we get hurt or get sick because sometimes lots of kids are sick at school and then we all get sick.

Thank you for Grandma and Grandpa because we love them so much and miss them when we don't see them enough.

Thank you for Mommy and Daddy who look after us and make us feel better when we hurt ourselves. We like when they play with us and don't look at their phones all the time.

Thank you for Mommy's and Daddy's strong shoulders so that we can get shoulder rides and be taller than everyone else.

Thank you for my paints so that I can make lots of **pictures** and give them to people as **presents**.

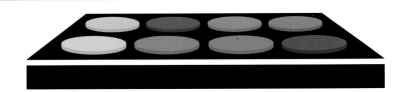

Thank you for my pets who play with me and also sit with me when they want to be scratched or hugged.

Thank you for cars, buses, and trains because they help us get to school and the shops when we need to buy food.

Thank you for all the countries in the world because there are seven billion people on planet earth and that's where they all live.

46

Thank you for swim lessons so that
I can swim by myself in the water.

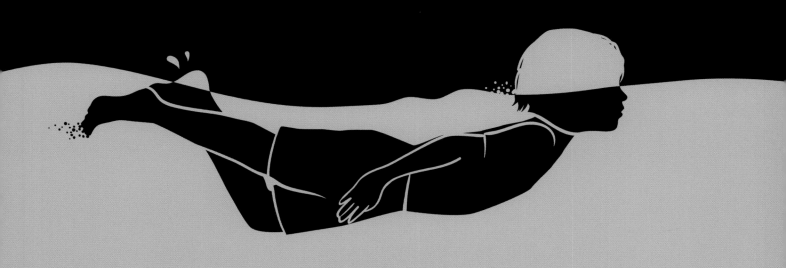

Thank you for video chat so we can speak to Grandma and Grandpa, even when they are living in a different country.

Thank you for the clouds and the rain that help the trees and plants grow and give drinks and bathwater to all the animals and birds.

Thank you for the **soil** that **helps** the vegetables **grow** so we can eat them and get **bigger** and have **healthy** bodies, and thank you for **worms** that help make the soil **good** for **plants** to grow in.

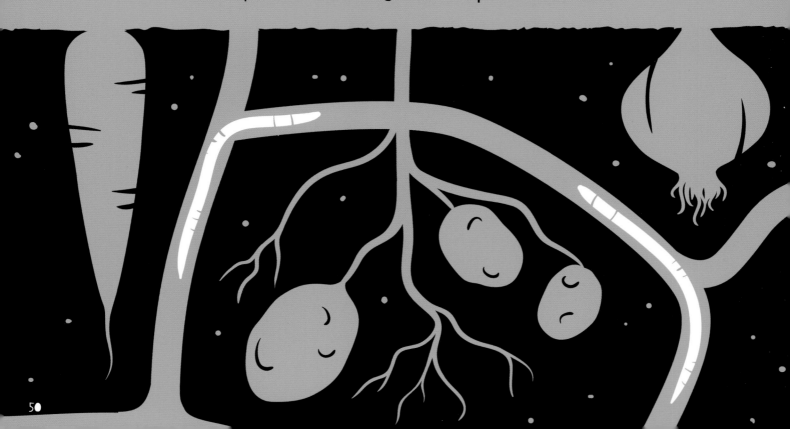

Thank you for the snow that cools down the earth and that we use to build snowmen and slide down hills on our sleds.

Thank you for Mommy who dances with us
in the kitchen and makes us laugh.

Thank you for people who don't use **plastic straws** because they are **bad** for the **planet**.

Thank you for planes that let us travel to see our family in different cities and different countries where they live.

Thank you for the wind that keeps us cool in the summer and that blows baby flowers to different places where they can grow.

Thank you for our mouths so we can eat and speak to each other. Some people can speak to each other by using their hands!

Thank you for making me patient when I keep trying to do something that doesn't work, like when I was learning to ride a bicycle and kept hurting myself.

Thank you for magic. Mommy and Daddy tell me that life is magic and sometimes I see it happen when I am thinking about my friends and then I see them at the park, and we are all surprised!

Thank you for everything we learn,
so that we know how to do lots of things
that make planet earth a better
place for everyone.

Thank you for my brothers and sisters who I love a lot, even when they make me angry. I know that we will always be friends even when I am seventy-one and I might have gray hair like a grandpa.

Thank you for charities because they give money and food to people who don't have any homes. It is good to collect money for them because then they can eat and get stronger.

Evening

Thank you for when I get out of the bath and Daddy or Mommy wraps me up really tight in a big towel and hugs and kisses me on my nose.

Thank you for my warm cozy bed
where I can sleep and dream.

Thank you for planet earth,
which feeds and protects us, and
for the planets that share our
solar system with us.

Thank you for the moon
that lights up the night sky
and helps move the oceans
forward and backward.

Thank you for my thank-yous that Daddy makes me say after I have a nightmare and I am too scared to go back to sleep.

It makes me think of happy things so that I forget my bad dream.

Thank you for our imaginations so we can play make-believe and think of made-up stories to tell each other.

Thank you for my breath,

especially when I am angry or upset and

Daddy tells me to breathe until I calm down a bit, like when I meditate.

Thank you for our memories so that we can remember all the fun times we have had in our lives.

Thank you for bedtime stories when we spend time with Mommy and Daddy and they tell us cool stories about trains or dragons or funny mice.

Thank you for my teeth so that I can chew
all my food before it goes into my belly.

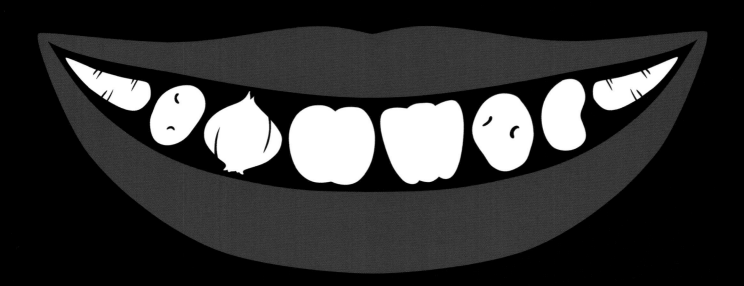

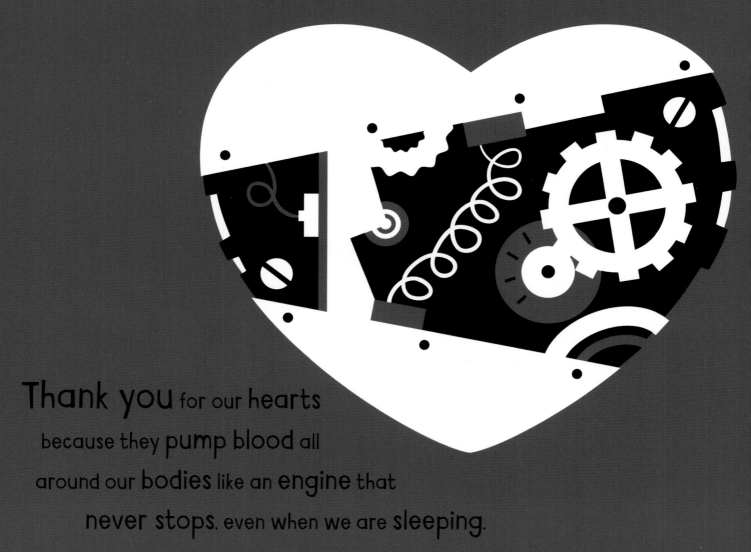

Thank you for our hearts
because they pump blood all
around our bodies like an engine that
never stops, even when we are sleeping.

Thank you for all the stars in the sky that look like sparkles at night and we can make wishes on them.

Thank you for our home where we can sleep and play
and be with our whole family and because it keeps us safe.

Thank you for electricity so that we can have **lights** in our **house** even when it is **dark** outside. so we can **see** each other and **read books** and play.

Thank you for meditation that helps our brains be calmer and that helps us to relax and to not get so angry.

Thank you for my dreams that show me magic
stories in my head like when I can fly.

Thank you for my guardians and angels because they look after us all and keep us safe. Angels are sometimes people who have died, like great grandpas and grandmas, and now they are in the stars looking after us.

Thank you for our lives.

Thank you for everything!

"Be content with what you have;
rejoice in the way things are.
When you realize there is nothing lacking,
the whole world belongs to you."

—*Lao-Tzu.*

Photo by Nina Clemente

About the Author

HSH Prince Alexi Lubomirski was born to a Peruvian-English mother and a Polish-French father. He grew up between Botswana, Oxford, and London. At the age of eleven, he was informed of his true ancestral heritage and aristocratic bloodline. Having not grown up in royal surroundings with all the trappings, he was the first of his family in five hundred years to have the title with none of the material evidence. Thanks to this displaced upbringing, and after much trial and error, he gradually succeeded in marrying his history with his present, managing to fulfill his role as the bearer of this title; and at the same time adapting the meaning, in this modern-day world, for him and his sons.

Apart from being primarily a husband and a father, Alexi Lubomirski is a world-renowned fashion photographer who has worked for several magazines, such as *Vogue* and *Harper's Bazaar*. Among other things, Lubomirski shot the official engagement and wedding portraits for HRH Prince Harry and Ms. Meghan Markle.

In 2014, he published *Princely Advice for a Happy Life*, a book written for his two young sons, on the virtues of behaving in a manner befitting a prince in the twenty-first century.

Lubomirski is also a global ambassador for the humanitarian charity Concern Worldwide, to which he donates all of his book's proceeds.

@alexilubomirski

Concern Worldwide is a nongovernmental, international, humanitarian organization dedicated to the reduction of suffering and working toward the ultimate elimination of extreme poverty in the world's poorest countries.

Since its foundation in 1968, Concern Worldwide—through its work in emergencies and long-term development—has saved countless lives, relieved suffering, and provided opportunities for a better standard of living for millions of people. It works primarily in the countries ranked in the bottom 40 of the United Nations' Human Development Report. Concern Worldwide implements emergency response programs as well as long-term development programs in the areas of livelihoods, health, HIV/AIDS, and education.

www.concernworldwide.org

@concernworldwideus

Acknowledgments

Thank you to my amazing literary agent, Anne Bohner, and also Patty Rice from Andrews McMeel for both believing in my little projects.

Thank you to the illustrator, Tracey Knight, who brought each "thank you" to magical life.

Thank you to all the incredible people who work at the charity Concern Worldwide for allowing me to attach this book to their cause and for doing the real heroic work!

I give thanks to my sons, Sole Luka and Leone, for motivating me every day to be a better man and a better role model for them, for showing me how love can inspire, and for dictating this book to me.

Lastly, I give eternal gratitude to, and for, my wife Giada, @ecoshaker, whose love guides me every day. I love you.

THANK YOU FOR MY DREAMS

Andrews McMeel Publishing
a division of Andrews McMeel Universal
1130 Walnut Street, Kansas City, Missouri 64106

www.andrewsmcmeel.com

19 20 21 22 23 RLP 10 9 8 7 6 5 4 3 2 1

ISBN: 978-1-4494-9742-2

Library of Congress Control Number: 2018963471

Made by:
Shenzhen Reliance Printing Co., Ltd
Address and Location of Manufacturer:
25 Longshan Industrial Zone, Nanling,
Longgang District, Shenzhen, China, 518114
1st printing—2/18/19

Editor: Patty Rice
Art Director: Julie Phillips
Designer: Diane Marsh
Production Editor: Dave Shaw
Production Manager: Tamara Haus

ATTENTION: SCHOOLS AND BUSINESSES
Andrews McMeel books are available at quantity discounts with bulk purchase for educational, business, or sales promotional use. For information, please e-mail the Andrews McMeel Publishing Special Sales Department: specialsales@amuniversal.com.